THE **GUIDE** TO BEATING **ANXIETY**
AND **GROUNDING YOURSELF**

CALM YOUR CHAOTIC MIND

UDAY JOSHI

*Nothing is permanent in this wicked
world — not even our troubles.*

Charlie Chaplin

Uday Joshi is an urbanite, a dreamer, and an adventurer, specialising in Digital Markering. With customer marketing engagement through user to business relationships, and a wild panoply of fields. Uday knows his trade when it comes to all things strategic planning and originality, but he especially focuses on providing a deeper human experience.

Uday first gained a Bachelor's degree in Marketing from the University of Middlesex and then went on to earn his Masters for Marketing Communication from the University of Westminster. Throughout these years, he experienced, like many other students, self-doubt, high anxiety, and fear of failure. As such, he has decided to share his experience with others and use it to teach people who are also struggling more about how they can relax and take advantage of all that life has to offer.

In fact, Uday now posts on a regular basis on his blog, sharing his insights regarding toxic positivity, managing perfectionism, healing old wounds and having the courage to keep going when things seem too difficult. He is particularly interested in helping others find themselves and find more empathy for other people.

A true believer that we either win or learn in any situation, he strongly believes in having a growth mindset, or a mindset that allows one to overcome any hard time in life. With this mindset, he has seen himself succeed in various parts of his life, hence why he is now working on bringing this message to others.

TABLE OF CONTENTS

HOW ARE YOU FEELING?

Anxiety: "a feeling of unease, such as worry or fear, that can be mild or severe".

This is the definition that one can find on the NHS' website, and the first definition to come up when you search for the word's definition. Throughout the past few years (as this book is being written in the Summer of 2021), we have been through significant anxiety-triggering events. The global pandemic has taken its toll on most of the general public's mental health. We are more depressed, less optimistic, and much more likely to feel extremely stressed about our achievements. After all, we have just gone through a solid year and a half of uncertainty. Thus, with very little control over what's to happen next, needless to say, many of us have become very well accustomed with this term – anxiety –, making it much more than just a buzzword.

We deal with hundreds of stressors every day. Perhaps you are in the middle of your Bachelor's degree and you are trying to figure out exactly what you want to be doing for the rest of your life. Maybe the life you had imagined for yourself is not working out as planned. Maybe you are stuck at home in a Covid-19 related lockdown and you feel like whatever is coming, you are not ready for. Perhaps your friends seem to be doing much better than you and you feel like you're being left behind. Whatever your source of pressure or stress is in life, it's something you can get a hold of. Whatever you are going through right now, you can find the calm within the chaos as long as you have the right tools to get there.

Anxiety has always been present. However, it has become a much more popular concept over the past few years because of how widespread it is. Not only this, but it is affecting all kinds of people located just about everywhere on this planet. It affects me too! It's a deep feeling that makes you wonder whether you are actually on the right path, or whether you are wasting your time. It's all the *What if?* thoughts that come into your mind at the most inconvenient moments. It's all the times you've thought *ugh, why is it that other people can just do these things like that without feeling like they're being judged the entire time? Or like some worst-case scenario is waiting to happen? Am I the only one thinking like this? What's wrong with me?*

No, there's nothing wrong with you. You just have anxiety. And it's something that can be changed. Instead of constantly feeling like you aren't sure of where you are going or what you are doing, you can work on yourself so you can focus on the things you have in your hands instead of the stressors that you are constantly dealing with. You can calm the chaos that is in your mind by letting yourself focus on the present and on what you can see and experience, instead of what's missing. My goal with this book is to help you achieve just that; first, by understanding what anxiety is and how it differs from regular stress, and second, by outlining the various ways you can control your anxious thoughts.

Throughout my life, I have been through significant anxiety-inducing situations. It's with these experiences that I was also able to understand that sometimes, getting past these feelings of anxiety can be as simple as doing some inner work. Whether you feel like you are lost in life, like there is constant pressure or like you really have no idea where to go, this book will help you take a minute and think about the rationality of all these worries. My goal throughout this book is to use the personal experiences I have dealt with to give you tips and tricks on getting past this anxiety. That's the real secret to getting over anxiety.

So, get ready for a journey that will take you from personal experiences to real, concrete advice on overcoming anxiety. Whether you are struggling with intrusive thoughts, are stressed about what's to come in your future, or you just generally feel an overwhelming sense of worry that you can't deal with, these are all things you can get over. You're not too young or too old to make a change in your life to make it what you really want it to be. You have the control and power to make your life what you'd like it to be, but for that, you also need to have mental clarity – and that's hard to find if you're anxious all the time! So, without further ado, let's get started.

CHAPTER ONE

DEFINING ANXIETY

Before we get into the details, it may be useful to define what anxiety is and how it differs from stress. More and more, we're seeing the former being used as a general term to describe any kind of stress you may be dealing with when the reality is that anxiety can, in fact, be overwhelming and debilitating. So, let's talk about what anxiety is like.

The word "anxiety" can mean any number of things. Generally speaking, anxiety is just a state of apprehension regarding something. It can also mean fear, worry, or excessive concern about everyday events or things. This is a common symptom of everyday life for people who have a general anxiety disorder – they worry about anything and everything, and most of the time, this worry is completely irrational. Sounds familiar?

Anxiety and stress are two aspects of the same coin, though in different words and different severity. Anxiety is simply the physical manifestation of stress. Stress is often caused by a recent event or occurrence that makes you tense or concerned about something: you can pinpoint the exact source of the negative emotion or the thing that makes you feel uncomfortable. On the other hand, if you experience worry or stress without a specific reason on a regular basis, it is called chronic anxiety.

General anxiety disorder, which affects millions of people, consists of frequent worrying about everyday problems or general events that don't cause stress for other people. You may be worried about money, health, work, family, and more, but when these worries hinder you from doing anything (i.e. when you end up completely avoiding doing anything to help your situation because you are overwhelmed by the feeling of stress), you are suffering from anxiety and not just stress. Chronic general anxiety disorder can lead to various sub-types of anxiety, such as agoraphobia (the fear of extremely crowded spaces), social anxiety, and so on. These can also worsen into fears such as the fear of traveling, of tight spaces, heights, water, germs, and others. Anxiety, when generalized, can make you feel like you are somewhat crazy! People around you may look at you like a mad man when you voice your concerns, and you may have a hard time shaking off the potential risks that you are anxious about.

When you are anxious, your heart rate, breathing, and your body's natural fight-or-flight response are triggered and/or increased. Because of this change, you may feel physically ill from being so stressed out. In order to reduce your anxiety, you need to learn to face your stresses head-on. When you face your fears and deal with them right away instead of avoiding them, you are able to gain control over your anxiety and reduce its effects on your body and mind.

Thus, anxiety is an intense feeling of fear which can vary from mildly anxious feelings to intensely fearful ones. It is a common, often overwhelming, feeling of worry that can be debilitating and difficult to cope with. Sufferers may experience irritability, muscle tension, insomnia, restlessness, difficulty concentrating, fatigue, nausea, headaches, dizziness, and even chest pain from this anxiety. Unlike stress, it completely takes over the rational aspect of decisions. For example, your heart rate may go completely through the roof if you even think about having to call your hairdresser to make an appointment. This could cause physical discomfort to the point where you may avoid going to the hairdresser's altogether.

Specific examples of anxiety disorders are phobias, panic disorders, separation anxiety, obsessive-compulsive disorder, and general anxiety disorder (GAD). Phobias are persistent and unreasonable fear of particular situations. Panic disorder is a sudden and overwhelming fear of danger, while obsessive-compulsive disorder is excessive and repeated obsessive thoughts and worry about specifics (it's more complex than that, but for now, we'll focus on generalized anxiety). General anxiety is the persistent and intense thought and concern about health, money, work, family, or one's performance, among many other things. As such, you may be intensely worried about any of these.

Stress is a normal part of our experience. However, when it becomes excessive and starts to interfere with daily activities, it can turn into a disorder characterized by unpleasant feelings of fear that doesn't go away, or anxiety – stress about something for no rational reason. These feelings are usually associated with something that could happen in the future – "what if" thoughts and worst-case scenarios.

Why Are We Anxious?

It's no secret that we are living in a world that's extremely fast-paced and one that barely gives us the time to take a breath and calm down here and there. We're constantly on the look-out for the next cool thing to be a part of, or the next important deadline that we need to meet. This never-ending feeling of "having something to do" or having expectations to meet is at the root of many individuals' anxiety for the simple reason that even when we don't have to *do* something, we feel like we *should* be doing something.

Aside from this, we also fear what we don't know or cannot control. Perhaps we are dealing with a situation that we aren't sure how to handle. Maybe you're worried about missing your flight, and even once you are boarded, you still worry about something happening that puts a hamper on your plans. External factors like work-related stress that is not taken care of properly, school-related stress, stress from your interpersonal relationship, financial stress or more global stress (e.g. about the state of politics in your country) can all lead to anxiety. Of course, unpredictable events are often at the root of a significant proportion of anxiety, including pandemics.

This isn't to say that your anxiety can be forgotten because it can be rationalized. Although you are stressed about certain events, if the fear you have of the worst-case scenario happening is taking over your capacity to live your daily life normally, you should be considering whether this anxiety has begun to take too big of a role in your life. Some stress is normal, but anxiety that is debilitating should be paid attention to promptly.

The Signs of Anxiety

If you've ever felt a creeping dread or anxiety as you prepare for a big social event, exam, or presentation, then you know symptoms of anxiety. Anxiety symptoms can make it difficult to concentrate, keep your mind clear, and prevent thoughts of worry from overtaking your thoughts. Many symptoms of anxiety are similar to symptoms of panic disorder. So what are the symptoms of anxiety that you should be on the lookout for, and how do these differ from symptoms of stress?

Stress is characterized by excessive physical and mental distress, whereas anxiety is usually accompanied by somatic, psychological, and behavioral symptoms. While under stress, some stressors may well be identified as a specific trigger, for example, a major academic test or presentation. With anxiety, however, some triggers are less obvious. For example, during times of conflict or when a person is anticipating a major change in his or her life, anxiety can manifest itself in varying ways. Some people become nervous or tense all the time, or even become anxious about the smallest things. Others may simply find themselves worrying or fretting over minor things such as a seemingly insignificant event.

Physical symptoms of anxiety include pounding heartbeats, nausea, sweating, cramps, dizziness, headaches, diarrhea, and fatigue. An intense fear of dread or danger compels a person to avoid these events – the mental symptoms therefore usually include a severe fear of something terrible happening and having a hard time rationalizing it. One of the symptoms of anxiety is excessive shortness of breath, or hyperventilation.

This occurs when there is insufficient oxygen in the bloodstream due to a physical limitation – your body feeling like it cannot get enough air. It's something you may know well as a panic attack.

Ultimately, if you feel like there is an impending danger, panic, or doom in many situations, the feelings you have are likely to be anxiety. If you are simply nervous but can pinpoint why, it is more likely to be caused by stress. In any case, there are ways for you to gain control over these feelings and to be more grounded whenever you feel overwhelmed by anxiety or stress.

Now that we have clearly established what anxiety is, let's jump right into the various reasons why you may feel anxious and how you can get past it. As mentioned in the introduction, my goal is to share my personal stories with you and in the meantime, give you tips and tricks based on what I have learned. So, let's get to it.

CHAPTER TWO

DO YOU FEAR THE UNKNOWN?

Are you scared about what's going to happen next? Are you worried about the things that are unknown to you, or perhaps the things that you cannot foresee happening? Whenever we have big events coming up, needless to say, we may be anxious to see what the outcome will be. Maybe you're seeing all your friends performing extremely well in university and in the meantime, you can't get yourself to get up before 11 AM on weekdays. Or, maybe you feel like there are so many opportunities lying ahead that you aren't even sure of where to start. Maybe you are constantly anxious about what's coming next, or what you could be doing instead of staying in bed, but you are too worried about the unknown and fearful of what *could* happen. Am I going to fail? What if it doesn't work? Is it even worth putting the time in if none of it is likely to work? The short answer? Yes!

What exactly is the fear of the unknown? Why do some people fear the unknown more than others do? And do the fears of the unknown really have any effect on the way that we live our lives? These are some of the questions that arise when we begin to explore our personal development journeys. Fear of the unknown can be defined as an unreasonable intense fear of unknown things or circumstances that might occur in the future, or the fear that we'll waste our time working on something that we are unsure will actually work out. Some people fear the unknown because they have an intolerance for uncertainty. This is especially true when the unknown has a potentially negative outcome, such as an accident happening or looking like a fool if failure happens.

One theory about why we feel such fear is that we are programmed to only go with the things we are certain of – it's a form of survival. The more uncertain a situation is, the more fear you feel. This alone could explain the universal source of anxiety and panic attacks! We, humans, are naturally afraid of the unknown because it is a part of our general adaptive process. It's what has kept us from dying in the past, and it's what makes sure that we don't end up in situations that could be otherwise harmful. The problem, however, is that we aren't exactly fighting lions anymore. Instead, we may be anxious about man-made stressors: not paying our taxes on time because we aren't sure of the process of doing such, missing out on an amazing job opportunity because we think we aren't qualified, and so on. This fear of the unknown can paralyze us into fear and it can make it extremely difficult for us to make sense of the chaos in our mind – making it even more difficult to experience mental clarity and peace of mind.

Going Solo

Let me tell you about the time I went skydiving on my own. Whenever you see videos of other people skydiving, you are already very much aware of the thrill and the adrenaline rush that it brings in. And yet, nothing can prepare you for what's to come. When I used to watch videos on skydiving to prepare myself for the experience, I did feel like I was ready for whatever was to come. Man, how wrong I was! Going on a solo skyjump was potentially the most testing and fear-inducing event

I've been through. The fact was that I had no idea what I was getting myself into, and yet, I still went ahead and jumped. Instead of letting my mind race and get lost in the various ideas and fears it could go through, I took a deep pause and focused on the present moment. No thinking of the worst case scenario, or thinking of the potential scenarios (the What Ifs). No, instead, I thought about the amazing experience I was about to experience. I was *mindful* of what I was going through. So, this is my first tip: whenever you struggle with anxiety about what *could* happen, don't let it hold you back. Instead, be mindful of what you are currently going through. Base yourself on what you know and what you are aware of, not what you don't know. Don't let something that you do not *not* know hold you back from experiencing great things. Don't let things that you have no idea about or cannot even contemplate stop your actions. This is called being *mindful*. Let's expand on that.

Mindfulness to Cope with Anxiety

Mindfulness is a state of becoming present. Basically, it entails being aware and awake to every moment without pre-judgment and with complete acceptance of everything that is happening around you. It is said that mindfulness increases your creativity as it helps you absorb ideas better instead of acting as a barrier to all opportunities lying in front of you (which is what the fear of the unknown does to your mind!). Mindfulness is also known to be a state of health as you are able to remain in the present instead of succumbing to anxiety.

Many health benefits may be gained by simply paying attention to your experience in the present. One of the most important benefits of mindfulness is that it helps you avoid distractions and instead puts you in a state of clarity that allows you to live in the moment and experience the sensations that arise without focusing on the negatives. Some people have said that mindfulness is like going on a spiritual healing fast. In fact, many people who say that mindfulness helps in improving their health do note that their physical well-being seems to improve and they have fewer illnesses and ailments as well. Your mental health and anxious feelings can indeed affect your physical health as we have noted, so it isn't too hard to imagine!

Mindfulness makes you think like this:

I am anxious because X thing might happen. Is there something I can do about it within the next five minutes?

No. So what can I do instead? I can focus on what I am living right now instead. I can appreciate the experience.

A thought is just a thought until you give it more power! Mindfulness is an essential quality of being alive. When you are fully present in your life, there is no room for anxiety to creep in. Stress and anxiety arise from our habitual response to events in our lives, so when you are mindful, you become calm and more relaxed instead of responding to every single stressor or perceived danger. You may experience stress from work, from home, or from social interactions with other people, and with mindfulness, you become able to stop these negative feelings before they even arise.

Mindfulness can be practiced in daily life. You don't have to meditate to obtain it, but you can certainly learn the benefits of mindfulness by doing meditation exercises. Mindfulness meditation is an exercise that helps you to tune into yourself and become aware of your body, mind, and world. Meditation cultivates self-awareness and helps you become more aware of your thoughts without judging them with your subconscious mind. It helps you realize that your worries are just that – worries – and that unless you can do something about them, it's not worth losing sleep over them. Learn a few mindfulness techniques as these can come in handy when you feel a ping of anxiety coming through!

A powerful way to practice mindfulness is with breath awareness meditation. Breathing exercises are a wonderful way to deepen your focus and awareness, because the more aware you are of your breathing, the easier it is to stay present in the moment. In this type of mindfulness, your goal is to become aware of your breath all the time, and not to get wrapped up in what is happening mentally. You want to just be aware of your breath as it comes and goes. This can be a challenge, because as you tend to focus on what is happening in your mind, sometimes sensations can become distracting. You can put a stop to that with mindful breathing – try it the next time you feel a sensation of worry coming over you!

Whenever you fear that something coming up is not controllable or that you cannot foresee what will happen, take a minute to stop and consider the facts. What do you know? What about the future? What about the unknown? What is truly so bad about not knowing what is about to happen? Is it all that dramatic? Most likely not! Using mindful breathing and focusing on the present by purposely bringing yourself back to what you can feel, hear, see, or even smell can bring you back from a ping of anxiety that's triggered by your fear that there is something you cannot control. Try it before you kick it!

Remember: a thought is just a thought. What you fear, what you are worried about or what you are worried about out of a lack of prediction is not dramatic. You can control it. You can choose to change the path of your thoughts and to control how you react to certain situations. The same way that I was able to throw myself into the sky even though I had no idea of what would happen and what the possibilities truly were, you can also get past the fear of the unknown.

Take a minute to think about times where you may have missed out on great opportunities because you were unsure of the potential outcome. Now, think about what *could* have been. What could you have done that's different? What kind of great outcomes have you potentially missed out on? Don't let this trigger more anxiety – instead, use it as fuel to force yourself to take the opportunity next time. If you get worried about the outcome because you can't predict it, you are holding yourself back from tremendous potential and success.

Don't let that happen! Do whatever you want to achieve, and use mindfulness to help yourself be grounded when you feel very stressed or anxious. On that note, let's now discuss another form of fear that has a similar effect on us: the fear of failure.

C H A P T E R   T H R E E

DO YOU FEAR FAILURE?

Life may offer us lemons, but even then, it's up to us to make lemonade out of them. And yet, a person with anxiety won't have the same path of thoughts as someone without it. Instead of just picking up the lemon and cutting it into halves to then extract the juice, a person with anxiety may think about the potential risk of picking up the knife and it slipping from their hand onto their foot. Or, they may think about how the lemon could slip from under their hand, slicing it open in the meantime. Can you relate?

Fear of failure can lead to negative self-talk which perpetuates negative thoughts about your own abilities and potential for success. The thoughts you have about yourself and your abilities can prevent you from taking advantage of opportunities. If you have negative self-talk, then you probably do not believe that you are talented enough, or you may think that only someone else will be able to achieve the success you would like.

The fear of failure is largely due to your beliefs about yourself– this, as well as your abilities, may keep you from taking action in a proactive manner. Your beliefs about yourself and your capabilities make it impossible for you to take advantage of new opportunities because you fear failing. Therefore, whenever you encounter a situation or opportunity that gives you a good chance at success, your mind and body work to convince you that the worst possible outcome is the only viable one. For instance, when you do a difficult task, your brain focuses on the negative consequences that will take place if you fail instead of looking at the positive side of things.

Now, my lemon metaphor does in fact have a purpose here. When we are too busy worrying about things not working out the right way or things ending up as failure, we may be so stressed that we don't even see the point in trying. This is where fearing failure, when combined with anxiety, can become toxic and can act as nothing other than a hurdle in our way to developing ourselves as individuals. Whatever struggles you have in life and no matter how chaotic your life might be, there is a way to take away this fear that you may fail. And once you can do that, you can do anything.

Get That 'U'

When I was in college, I ended up getting an "U" – an undefined grade in the system I was in. I was extremely inspired to take on the world of business and I learned tremendously more on that specific day than I ever did on any previous day. I realized that I knew exactly where I wanted to take my career. I was given another chance! After this undefined grade, I realized that perhaps I wasn't doing the right thing. Maybe what I thought I wanted to do my entire life wasn't really for me after all. I had always thought of business as being the *end-all* choice – the only choice I could consider. I would watch shows about successful businessmen and women, and Youtube videos on how people made it in business. And then, I realized that perhaps I had been living with a perspective of the world that was closed to only what I was able to see – tunnel vision, as you may call it.

Whatever was going on in my life, I thought it was the best potential scenario because that's all I was focused on. I was so focused on following that past that I would not consider other options which perhaps presented a risk of failing or of falling flat on my face a few times that I just stuck to what I knew and what I was certain would work – until it didn't.

That's when I changed my path and started to work on a different path. I began my Bachelor's degree in Marketing and I instantly felt that I needed to be doing more. I then got into a Master's degree in marketing communications, diving deep into the subject and consistently learning, never giving up. I need to shake the failure off to be able to take a step. That takes a lot of work! It takes the ability to set your ego aside and realize that what you thought would work didn't, after all. It makes you realize that sometimes, even the things that you were completely certain would work in your favour do not always work out. So, you need to be able to take a leap of faith and have to be able to step forward and try things out, even if it means that you might fail.

It takes resilience! It takes the ability to be emotionally intelligent enough to understand that letting yourself fall down and just giving up completely won't lead you anywhere. Instead, capitalize on your strengths and do not let the fear or anxiety that you'll fail by trying something new get to you. Get into that growth mindset where all failures are learning opportunities. It's what resilience is made of and it's what helps you get past failure. That mindset provides calm in the storm and order in the chaos because you can take on any difficulty and make it a learning curve instead of the end of a difficult path.

The fear of failure is paralyzing. It can make us do nothing and thus unwilling to move forward. When we let fear stop us from moving forward, we are prone to miss out on some truly great opportunities along the way. Fear of failure keeps us from exploring areas of our lives we might otherwise take advantage of. When paired with anxiety, it can truly make you stop living and can make you simply exist instead. You have a fear of failure because you expect failures to occur regularly. Therefore, if you think you are going to fail, then you probably are. So instead of imagining that you will fail, think of all the times you've overcome a certain fear or challenge and won. It doesn't matter how big or small – you just need to think of how often the "best case" scenario took place instead of the worst-case scenario. This will give you hope, motivation and help you continue to build on your personal development in regards to the anxiety you may be feeling. Instead of seeing failure as the end-all and be-all of life, see it as just another learning experience. You will come through this fear of failure, stronger and smarter because you learned how to conquer fear and move on.

Work on Resilience

Resilience is one of the important life skills that we can learn. It's all about being able to bounce back after being affected by adversity and change. Resilience theory describes the ways around how individuals deal with and adapt to things such as change, adversity, loss, danger, and risk. However, resilience can also mean being resilient in the face of failure, making changes, and adaptation to different circumstances.

The concept of resilience has different meanings for different people. For some, resilience is the ability to survive and work even under extraordinary personal, economic, political, or environmental conditions. For others, resilience is the ability to change with the times and remain adaptive. Still, others define resilience in terms of overcoming risks and adapting to new situations.

Resilience is the ability to change and adapt to changes in your environment as well as the external and internal world. Your resilience may be impacted by trauma, burnout, depression, distress, loss, difficulties in your private life, or change itself. In other words, the extent to which each of us is resilient depends fully on the things we have experienced and how these have built us.

Resilience relates to how you handle stress and negative emotions in everyday life. If you are able to manage stress and change your behaviors in order to avoid the negative impacts of this stress and these emotions, you are more likely to be very resilient and be better able to bounce back from difficult and stressful situations. You should hence make time to focus on learning healthy ways to deal with difficult times in your life, such as you are doing right now reading this book! Ultimately, the extent to which you are resilient will depend on all kinds of circumstances. If you were faced with many challenges when you were younger, chances are you have learned to naturally resist and stand back up whenever it happened. Maybe you went through trauma that changed your perspective of challenges and difficult times forever. Whatever it is, think about how fast you can get back up from adversity. Is it something you should work on, or do you consider yourself a pretty resilient person?

When looking at resilience, it's important to understand that it is not about ignoring your feelings, changing your personality, or stuffing your brain with so many "happy" thoughts that you feel like you're constantly putting up a mask, even when things are going wrong. Resilience is a skill that can help you change your perspective on stressful events. For example, instead of hiding your emotions, you would know how to navigate through them without letting them affect your overall productivity and capacity to function the same as on any other day. You have to be able to observe and know what is going on without getting caught up in your emotions – don't get me wrong, it's normal to feel and to be upset. However, it's key to know how to keep them under control so you don't fall down everytime something less than favourable happens to you. This key point is similar to emotional intelligence, the next item on our list of skills to take up.

Emotional Intelligence

When we say emotional intelligence, we are talking about a set of mental and emotional processes which determine one's ability to interact successfully with others – in other words, it's how well you can deal with your emotions and those of others so you aren't affected terribly whenever hardship comes up. It's especially helpful when you are dealing with anxiety because it helps you regulate your feelings and emotions, making it easier to understand why you might be feeling anxious. It helps you be in touch with yourself and your reactions, helping you understand your triggers and therefore what you can do to avoid them. Also called "EQ", it is the set of psychological processes and traits that lead you to have more control over how you feel and react to certain situations.

Emotionally intelligent people have a special capacity for noticing and regulating their emotional states. This ability is what is called mindfulness – interesting, right? Mindfulness, as we have established, is about being fully present in the moment: looking deeply at yourself, at others, and at the world around you to understand your reactions. Thus, being emotionally intelligent also requires you to be mindful about your circumstances.

Our third ability, aside from EQ and mindfulness, is emotional awareness. Those who are highly emotionally aware tend to know how to handle themselves and others. They also have an ability to better understand and manage their emotions, therefore not falling down or just avoiding challenges because they fear failing. They have an increased sense of well-being, and they tend to have better relationships with themselves and their ability to succeed.

When combined, all three help you to see failure as something that may happen but not something dramatic. In other words, it's what gets you to see that even if there are worst case scenarios and even if they *could,* theoretically-speaking happen, it wouldn't be the end of the world. If it does happen, you'll learn from it and you'll simply go forward in life. That's the core idea behind the growth mindset.

Growth Mindset

Cultivating the growth mindset is all about taking growth and the achievement of goals as cumulative steps when learning new things. We must never give up, even when things get tough or there is no end in sight. We must simply try the best we can with what we have, and move on if we fail – but not without learning from the experience beforehand. In this way, we are developing the mindset of a person who knows that even when things get tough there will always be an end result worth working for, even when others may want to give up instead. The growth mindset is therefore a combination of emotional intelligence and resilience.

A big part of cultivating the growth mindset is to know your strengths and weaknesses. You must recognize your ability and know what steps you need to take to improve upon those abilities. When it comes to calming the chaos in your mind, you'll see that this mindset helps tremendously. Why? Because you see that mistakes are part of life and learning from them is what gives us the motivation to continue moving forward. Instead of seeing the worst case scenario as the end of the road for you, you only see it as an opportunity to grow as a person. Therefore, adopting this mindset helps you put things in perspective. You start to understand that, well, SO WHAT! if things don't work out? Things will always settle back down. Worst case scenario, you'll need to work a bit harder to get over that mistake. Ultimately, these mistakes should not stop us from continuing on our path the same way that I did not let that undefined grade stop me. Instead, I realized that I could use it to realize the right path for me, and now, I am in the right place. And so what if I end up disliking where I am? I can always change things up to make them fit my new vision. Mistakes and missteps, or failure, should become reminders that we need to continue to strive for greater achievement. Once we are willing to embrace our mistakes and learn from them, growth is a very natural thing and anxiety in regards to the potential failures we may face only become another factor in the equation – not the deciding one.

The growth mindset is about allowing new experiences to teach you something new. It's not about avoiding your mistakes, it's about owning up to your mistakes and being able to use them to your advantage throughout life without letting yourself be completely overwhelmed if something doesn't work out the way it was supposed to. That can be extremely anxiety-triggering, but it's with this mindset that you'll begin to see the triviality of certain failures. Mistakes are a part of life and understanding that sometimes these things are unavoidable only makes them easier to deal with. Once you get to that mindset, you're all set when it comes to dealing with potential failure. Don't allow anxiety to hold you back – get in a mindset that can push you to keep going forward instead. But for that, you need to be present.

CHAPTER FOUR

BE PRESENT

Whenever I think about the various kinds of sources of stress in anyone's life, a few automatically come to my mind. For example, I think of social media. This relatively new form of communication started out as a way to show others what we were up to, or in some cases just to post a few pictures here and there. And yet, it has completely changed and evolved into something that may be doing more harm than anything else for some people. Don't get me wrong – it's a great way to connect with people. Through social media, you can speak to other people, see what they're busy doing, and see in real-time what fun things others are up to. But now, re-read that with some sad or thriller music in the back of your head. It's not all flowers, is it?

Sure, we get to see what other people do, but that also does have a bad impact on certain people. For example, it might make the well-known "fomo" (fear of missing out) worse. Social media has become somewhat of a hub on which certain people focus all their attention when it comes to showing off what they do, what they have, and how much they have achieved. Of course, it can have its great sides, especially when we want to celebrate something or show off an achievement we are proud of. On the other hand, it has also created somewhat of a fake reality in which people share what they *want others to see of them*, instead of what they are actually going through. For example, maybe you are spending the summer feeling bad about yourself and your "vacation" from uni because others are all in the south of Italy living their lives on the beach with endless, all-inc drinks while you're sitting and working to make some money for the next academic year. Or, perhaps you are looking at the pictures of people who used to go to your highschool, feeling like no matter what you have achieved thus far, the others have *clearly* done a lot more than you. And here you go again – that anxiety ping. Why isn't my life like this? Why do they all seem so happy and in the meantime, I'm stuck inside hating my 9-to-5 job? Why can't I also go to Italy?

And yet, there's another side of the story you aren't getting. Those friends of yours in the south of Italy? Although their Instagram story may be showing an amazing vacation, they're also extremely nervous and feel dependent on their parents because they can't afford it alone. Once they're back in town for uni, they're also going to be extremely stressed about their finances for that reason while you'll be over the moon. The friends from high school who made it far? They have the imposter syndrome, just like you. They feel like whatever they are doing, it's never enough and they just can't get anything right. So, although all of their social media accounts may show something completely different or something interesting – you never really know what other kinds of issues they're going through on the other end! In other words, you never know if they may also be struggling with anxiety, for example. If you base your own expectations of yourself on what you see others doing, such as always wanting to be better at something or always wanting to be better in the future, you're likely to only push your anxiety further for no reason. What you see on social media is only what *others want you to see.* In most cases, it's a completely unrealistic representation of life covered by filters and people who all try to show that they're happy even if they're completely dissatisfied with their lives. So, why let yourself feel worse about yourself or be anxious based on a fake representation of life? What if, instead, you could focus on being as present as possible?

Being in the *Now*

Take a deep breathe.

Whether you meditate, practice yoga, practice being mindful, or engage in other types of spiritual activities, being present is essential. Being fully focused and mindful means being open to your own experiences and simply appreciating that this is your reality – this is what you are doing, this is who you are, and you are at the right place in this very moment. Being present is much easier than being distracted, stressed, depressed, or worried, and it will eventually lead you to a happier you that isn't focused on what you could be if you were this person, or if you were doing that cool other thing. Even if meditation doesn't directly help you with these goals, it will certainly help you get into the right mindset so you can get to them, as will being fully focused and mindful during the way you live each and every moment. Don't focus too much on what others do: it doesn't help you, but instead, it makes you question whether you could be doing something else and whether you're in the right place. You guessed it, it only helps to increase your anxiety.

Cognitive Behavioural Therapy – Take Control of Your Thoughts

In most cases, you're likely to feel like you are overwhelmed with thoughts. This is usually what's at the root of anxiety. You think about all the things that could happen or should be happening, and in the meantime, you forget to focus on what's going on in the present. This is where a specific technique, called Cognitive Behavioural Therapy (or CBT for short), can help. It invites you to re-wire your thoughts so they don't stop you from doing great things out of fear, and instead, pushes you to take chances.

Cognitive behavioral therapy is an innovative psychotherapy technique that aims at improving emotional health by changing distorted thoughts and behaviours. It has been found to be highly effective in treating depression, social anxiety disorders, phobias, panic disorders, eating disorders, performance anxiety, alcohol and drug addiction, post-traumatic stress disorder, insomnia, obsessive-compulsive disorders, and many more. CBT aims to change cognitive behaviours and distortions, improve your capacity to self-care, regulate your emotions, adjust your behaviour, and improve your relationships.

CBT aims to change distorted thoughts and behaviours by addressing the root causes of emotional problems and preventing relapse. This therapy can also help you manage stress and anxiety. It aims to increase awareness, improve understanding, increase your ability to alter negative thoughts and behaviours, reduce risky behavior, and improve response in social situations so that you have more control over how you react to certain situations. CBT is a structured approach that teaches you how to think and act in a way that reduces negative emotions and fears, which is why it has been so helpful for those who struggle with anxiety. It helps you figure out what's the driving force behind your anxiety, making it a lot easier to change what needs to be changed to start feeling more in control of your reactions to events. This is something you can do with a therapist or on your own. For example, you can do CBT by doing the following:

Whenever anxiety pops up, question the source of the thought. What is the source? Is it rational? What brought you to this outcome? Is it accurate? Is this a negative thinking pattern that you have observed many times in your life? Do you have specific behaviours that you think need to be changed to alleviate anxiety and stress?

By using this kind of introspection, you can start to better understand why you may have certain reactions to specific events, hence making it much easier to then control those emotions when you have anxious thoughts or reactions!

Self-Awareness

Self-awareness refers to being aware of various aspects of one's self such as thoughts, feelings, attitudes, and traits. In essence, self-awareness is an emotional state where you understand yourself for all that you have to offer: your strengths, your weaknesses, and so on. It helps you deal with anxiety because you gain the capacity to understand why you have anxiety and therefore how you can avoid these triggers. Alongside the other tools we've discussed so far, from emotional intelligence to being mindful, self-awareness is an important tool to have in your bag. It is crucial that you become aware of your thoughts and feelings to be able to control them and avoid negative self-talk and behaviors. When you are self-aware, you can make changes to improve upon self-defeating patterns.

Self-awareness is hence something to work on if you've been struggling with being present. For example, whenever I am with my family or with friends, I make sure to focus on where I am at that very moment. I ensure that I am fully focused on them and on what I am doing at that very moment instead of focusing on just about anything else. I turn my phone around so I don't let notifications distract me. I let everything aside other than what I am doing right then and there. Do I need to be on my phone while I'm out with them? Of course not! Does looking at my social media to see what others are doing make me feel like I might be missing out on other stuff? Sometimes, yes! So, I choose to be fully present instead. I don't let my mind be scattered around, and instead, I focus on the now.

On that note, this brings us to the end of this chapter. As part of our final section, we will be discussing being kind to ourselves, avoiding limiting beliefs, and caring for ourselves with kindness and empathy.

CHAPTER FIVE

BE KIND TO YOURSELF
(AND OTHERS)

Anxiety, at the end of the day, happens when you have high expectations either for yourself or for your life (or both!). It can happen if you're scared about what's to come, or if you're worried that you won't be able to achieve much unless you put in an enormous amount of work. It can also happen if you feel like you'll only succeed if you achieve more than everyone else around you. Burnout usually starts this way: you're so anxious about not doing enough, succeeding enough, or *being* enough that you end up doing way too much and overworking yourself. And then, once you've worked yourself to the bone, you feel like nothing is working out even if you have no energy left to work things through. So what can you do instead? Be kind to yourself, for one.

What Does it Mean?

What is even kindness in this context? I would argue that it refers to whatever you feel makes the most sense to you. Do you show your kindness through acts of service? Or maybe through encouragement, gestures of affection, or generosity? Your definition of kindness is key here: it's what will make you feel like you're more in control. By being kind to others, the purity you feel also refreshes you with goodness and it gives you more strength to keep going, even when you are facing troubles. Kindness starts with yourself! It means treating yourself, using self-care, and caring for yourself enough that you treat and talk to yourself the same way you would want others to talk to you.

Kindness or self-compassion is one way we can learn empathy for ourselves and hence, later on, for others. Self-compassion is a kind of inner strength that allows us to identify with others and their unique feelings. When you are kind to yourself, you also tend to be kind to others. Thus, self-compassion helps us to gain empathy for others too.

Empathy is kind of like a universal solvent; it's what makes everything balanced and healthy. But not everyone has empathy for themselves and those around them, as painful as that can be. If you feel alienated from your family, your friends or other people, or if you are struggling with deep conflicts within your own life, then empathy for yourself is an important part of building healthy relationships. This lack of empathy for yourself could very well be at the root of your anxiety!

When we are empathizing with others, we are taking the role of looking into their eyes, feeling their pain, listening to their fears and hopes, appreciating their uniqueness, understanding their aspirations and goals, learning to respect them and their choices, as well as valuing the time they share with us. Basically, empathy involves "watching without being watched" - watching another person as they do what they do, without turning the feeling or the conversation around to fit our needs. On the other hand, you also need to have empathy for yourself in this journey – use this empathy to spend time on yourself to better understand the source of your anxiety and hence how you avoid it.

Empathy, however, is *not* sympathy. When we sympathize, we offer understanding and respect from afar. On the other hand, with empathy, we imagine the depth of the emotional state they are in and we relate to it. For this, we need to pay attention to them properly. We need to give them our real attention and need to show them that we are aware of their feelings and need to know what they expect of us – this requires emotional intelligence. It'll take time because we live in a high-paced world, but it's worth taking the time.

We may also struggle to give others or ourselves sympathy. If we feel threatened by a situation or a person's feelings, we may struggle to show empathy. Or, we may feel judgemental about a person's action, therefore making it difficult to show them that we care about their negative feelings. So, be real about how you feel. Imagine yourself in their position. And finally, forgive yourself and others, whatever the situation is.

Being empathetic towards others brings you a good feeling inside, one that brings more happiness and sun into your life. That's a great way of feeling less anxious and nervous about your situation and instead, being more present in your current situation.

Avoid Limiting Beliefs

Limiting beliefs are beliefs, ideas, or attitudes that limit one's potential. They typically have an adverse affect on your life, because by preventing you from progressing and rising on a personal and professional front, they prevent you from being able to enjoy all that life has to offer. Most times, limiting beliefs are subconscious thoughts that act as a defense mechanism against potentially lower or negative feelings (i.e. frustration, sadness, anger, disappointment with yourself). If you assume that you can't do something, you might just make yourself feel better by already preparing yourself for the disappointment.

First off, limiting beliefs aren't really "beliefs" at all. Rather, they are self-limiting thoughts that can keep you from taking action in the direction you'd like to go. For instance, limiting beliefs about your talents can keep you from getting things done because they make you wonder whether something is even worth trying out. Or, limiting beliefs about money can keep you from living a financially secure, peaceful life. They're not real, but limiting beliefs can still hold you back from achieving the life you want. Thus, they're quite powerful!

So, how do you deal with limiting beliefs? Well, one of the best ways to deal with them is to focus on your emotional intelligence instead. Emotionally intelligent people are nearly always in control of their emotions, which means that they always have the power to move ahead and regulate themselves when they notice that their thoughts are not conducive to good results. They don't get sidetracked by negative thoughts – instead, they know when to rationalize things. And what's more, their emotions are always running free and clear - which means that they know how to move forward even when there's an obstruction or a barrier in their way. Ultimately, this emotional awareness can help you feel a lot more in power of your beliefs. Whenever you realize that you are supporting any kind of negative thinking, throw it right out of your mind and replace it with positivity.

By changing these limiting beliefs, you'll give yourself the power to move forward on a different path. And the good news is that it doesn't take much effort or even thought to change your limiting beliefs - you just need to make the choice to do it. Once you make that choice, it will be easier for you to create the life you want. As cheezy as it sounds, it's true. You need to hold yourself accountable for the thoughts you have. They are just thoughts!

Indulge in Self-Care

The final point I want to make is that self-care is something you should also be putting effort in. Self-care, unlike what many think of it, is not always about putting on a face mask and doing your nails. Self-care, for example, if taking care of the things that are stressing you out solidly. For example, that might mean making sure that you are doing your laundry before the week starts so you don't end up having to wear dirty underwear the first few days. It might also mean cleaning your house properly, or setting up a workout plan. Self-care does not have to be glamorous to be considered "self-care". The goal of self-care is to do the things you need to get done to make sure that you feel good in your body. It is a series of activities or a routine that you implement in your day to day life just so you can decrease your amount of stress. It can be a routine that helps you feel less anxious because you get to simply follow a sequence of events that you feel comfortable with. We, human beings, are creatures of nature and we enjoy repetition. We like predictability. So, if you feel anxious because you cannot plan things or have control over them, implement a routine that fulfills that need for you.

Self-care strategies are designed to enhance your mental and physical well-being. When you engage in a well-balanced self-care plan, you are making sure that both your mental and your physical wellbeing are taken care of and therefore that you enjoy more calm in the chaos happening in your mind. A mental well-being plan focuses on the aspects of your life that influence how overwhelmed you may be with the tons of responsibilities you have. Meanwhile, a physical well-being plan focuses on the physical aspects of your life, such as eating better and exercising more. By taking care of both aspects of your life, you ensure the continuation of your physical health and the promotion of mental health that helps you finally be in control of anxiety.

So, give yourself what you need. Get a routine that works for you. Take care of yourself, and be kind to yourself. It'll make a world's difference.

I BELIEVE IN YOU

Anxiety can be debilitating. It can make you feel like whatever you are doing, you are never really doing enough. And yet, with all that we have been going through as a society, we continue to support practices and mindsets that reinforce this anxiety. Why is that? And why can't we simply appreciate the fact that we each have our own strengths and weaknesses? Being anxious over how well others are doing or what *we* are not doing does nothing for us other than bring negativity.

Ultimately, this was the goal for this book: to tell you that no matter what happens, everything will be okay. Perhaps you are trying to find your career and you are constantly stressed. Maybe you aren't so sure of where you are headed. But after all, what's the worst that can happen? Millions of other people are in your situation – no matter what your Instagram feed may tell you. You are not alone, and you have the tools available to help you deal with these challenges.

Go skydive solo, learn from a bad grade and grow into a more resilient person. Improve your emotional intelligence and adopt a growth mindset. Do whatever you feel is best for you, but do something. I believe in you!

Sincerely,

Uday Joshi

Made in the USA
Las Vegas, NV
13 January 2024